FACT-O-PEDIA

MAMMALS AND PRIMATES

Published in Moonstone
by Rupa Publications India Pvt. Ltd 2023
7/16, Ansari Road, Daryaganj
New Delhi 110002

Sales centres:
Prayagraj Bengaluru Chennai
Hyderabad Jaipur Kathmandu
Kolkata Mumbai

Copyright © Rupa Publications India Pvt. Ltd 2023

All rights reserved.
No part of this publication may be reproduced, transmitted,
or stored in a retrieval system, in any form or by any means,
electronic, mechanical, photocopying, recording or otherwise,
without the prior permission of the publisher.

P-ISBN: 978-93-5702-303-0
E-ISBN: 978-93-5702-313-9

First impression 2023

10 9 8 7 6 5 4 3 2 1

This book is sold subject to the condition that it shall not,
by way of trade or otherwise, be lent, resold, hired out, or otherwise
circulated, without the publisher's prior consent, in any form of binding
or cover other than that in which it is published.

Contents

Introduction	6
Evolution	8
Characteristics - I	10
Characteristics - II	12
Placental Mammals	14
Great Apes	16
Gibbons	18
Flying Mammals: Bats	20
Wild Dogs	22
Wild Cats	24
Hoofed Mammals	26
Elephants	28
Giraffes	30
Giant Pandas	32
Rodents	34
Marsupials	36
Different Marsupials	38
Marine Mammals	40
Monotremes	42
Glossary	44
Answers	46
Introduction	48
Types of Primates	50
Lemurs	52

Lorises	54
Tarsiers	56
Monkeys	58
Capuchin and Squirrel Monkeys	60
Woolly, Spider and Howler Monkeys	62
Baboons	64
Mandrills and Drills	66
Macaques	68
Colobuses, Langurs and Doucs	70
Apes	72
Gorillas	74
Chimpanzees	76
Orangutans	78
Gibbons	80
Siamangs	82
Threat to Primates	84
Glossary	86
Answers	88

MAMMALS

Introduction

Mammals are a class of warm-blooded vertebrates that includes humans. Horses, elephants, cows, sheep, cats and dogs are some other examples. Mammals are one of the oldest species on Earth. There are more than 5,500 living species of mammals, varying in size, form and habitat. In spite of the differences in their physical features, their anatomy is very similar. All mammals have hair on their body, breathe

through lungs and have a four-chambered heart. However, some, such as naked mole rats and whales, have lost much of their hair. Most females give birth to young ones and feed them with their own milk. There are some mammals known as 'monotremes' that lay eggs. The platypus is one such mammal.

Evolution

Mammals evolved during the Triassic Period along with the first dinosaurs. The earliest mammals were very small and shrew-like. The primitive mammals were very different from those that we see today. Mammals have passed through various stages of evolution. Fossil evidences show that they evolved from primitive reptiles.

Earliest mammals

The ancestry of mammals could be traced to the age of dinosaurs, around 210 million years ago. The earliest known mammals were tiny creatures the size of a shrew. They were known as *Sinodelphys*. They were among the different lineages of mammals that emerged at this time. However, for a long time, mammals could grow no larger than a cat due to the dominance of dinosaurs. After the disappearance of dinosaurs, mammals evolved to become more diverse.

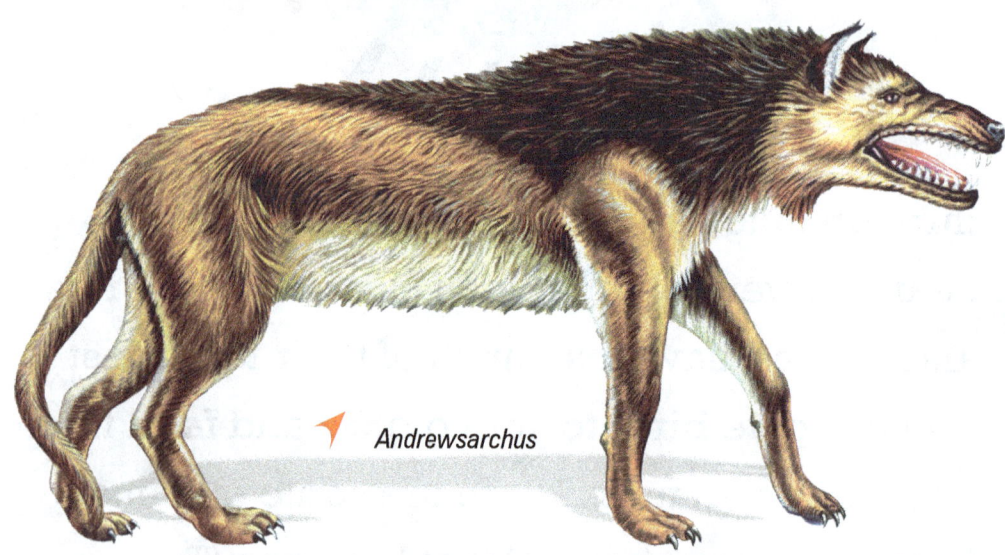

Andrewsarchus

Name any of the early mammals.

A long lineage

Jawless fish were one of the first complex animals to have evolved. They first appeared during the Cambrian Period of the Paleozoic Era. They were followed by the evolution of bony fish, which appeared some time between the mid-Ordovician and the late Devonian periods. Thousands of years later, insects and plants started gaining dominance over land. Eventually, some fishes developed legs and lungs and moved to land. These new animals were the earliest amphibians. This happened during the late Devonian and early Carboniferous Periods. During the late Carboniferous Period, another group of animals—the modern-day reptiles—also appeared. Some reptiles went on to evolve into some exceptionally large animals. During the late Carboniferous Period, the first mammal-like reptiles known as 'pelycosaurs' evolved. They, along with therapsids and cynodonts, were the ancestors of mammals. The first true mammals evolved from the cynodonts.

> **Facts**
> - The Andrewsarchus lived between 45 and 36 million years ago, is a mammal.
> - Cynodonts—carnivorous reptiles that lived during the late Permian and Triassic Periods—had most characteristics of mammals but they probably laid eggs.

Sinodelphys

Characteristics - I

Every animal has certain characteristics that enable them to survive in their environment. Animals of each group possess similar characteristics, some of which are visible while some others are not. Some clearly visible features of mammals are hair, mammary glands and their limbs.

Warm-blooded

Mammals are warm-blooded, endothermic animals. They are capable of regulating their body temperature according to their need. They generate heat by converting the food they eat into energy. When the temperature of their surrounding environment rises, their sweat glands secrete sweat to the skin surface. This helps to remove heat by the process of evaporation. Being warm-blooded is advantageous for mammals in very cold habitats such as the Arctic and mountain tops.

Facts

- A unique feature found only in mammals is a sheet of muscle and tendon known as diaphragm, which divides the body cavity into two parts.
- Sea otters have the thickest fur coat of all mammals. They have more than 100,000 hairs per sq cm of their skin.

Dentary

One of the features that differentiate vertebrates, such as birds, reptiles and amphibians, from mammals is that mammals have a single lower jaw bone that is attached directly to the skull. This bone holds the teeth of the lower jaw and is thus referred to as 'dentary'. In the other vertebrates, the dentary does not attach to the skull directly, and is one of the many bones in the lower jaw. The structure of the lower jaw in mammals provides them with a powerful bite, which helps them to rip off and chew their prey.

Movement

All mammals evolved from four-legged ancestors. However, over a long period, different mammals have evolved to have different ways of movement. There are some mammals like bats that can even fly. However, most advanced groups of mammals are bipedal. Most mammals are still quadrupeds, while swimming is the only way to move around for some.

Hair

All mammals have their body at least partially covered with hair at some point during their life. Their hair perform several functions such as protecting the skin and providing it insulation, camouflaging from enemies and providing warmth. Some mammals such as sea otters have two layers of hair: The inner layer has soft, fine hair that provides warmth; the outer layer has stiff hair to give shape to the coat. Hair on a mammal's body can be in the form of thick fur, quills, whiskers or even horns. Some mammals such as whales have hair only in the early stages of growth.

Are whiskers a form of hair in mammals?

Characteristics - II

Mammals have some unique characteristics which differentiate them from the other classes of animals. Some of these are a four-chambered heart, three middle-ear bones and mammary glands that produce milk for baby mammals.

Three middle-ear bones

The middle ear of mammals has three bones—malleus, incus and stapes, which are commonly known as the hammer, anvil and stirrup. These bones are a unique feature in mammals since no other animal group has them. These bones help mammals in hearing by transferring sound waves from the eardrum to the inner ear.

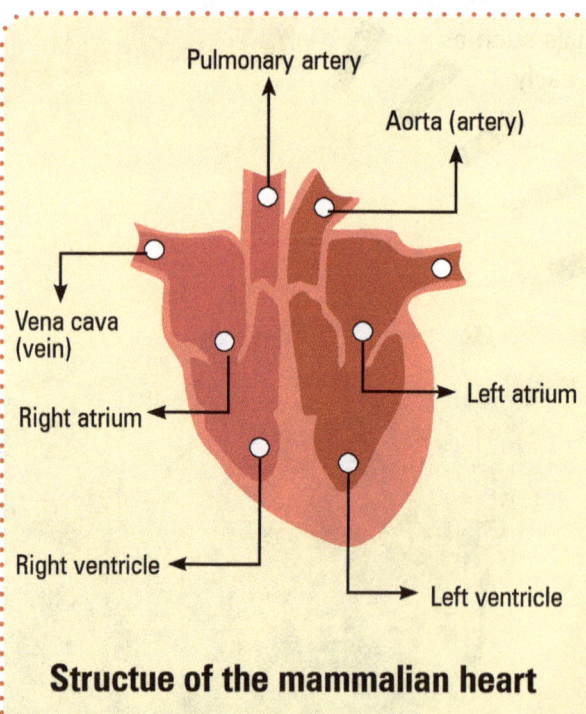

Structue of the mammalian heart

Heart

Mammals have a four-chambered heart. A four-chambered heart is highly efficient. The chambers for receiving fresh and deoxygenated blood are separate in four-chambered hearts. This ensures that the two bloodstreams do not mix, which further ensures greater muscle activity and the ability to maintain constant body temperature. Apart from mammals, birds also have four-chambered hearts.

Reproduction and mammary glands

Most mammals give birth to live young ones and the baby mammal grows inside the mother until they are born. The new born babies are fed on the mother's milk. The milk is secreted by the mammary glands in females. The milk is composed of proteins, lipids, sugars and water and is the primary source of food for newborns.

Facts

- The cerebrum is relatively larger than the rest of the brain in some higher mammals such as primates.
- The Cenezoic Era, the current era (65 million years ago until the present day) is often referred to as the Age of Mammals.

What is the current era known as?

Placental Mammals

There are three types of mammals: monotremes, marsupials and placental mammals. Placental mammals have a placenta in their body, which helps in the exchange of nutrients and wastes between the mother's blood and that of the fetus. A well-developed placenta in the placental mammals facilitates a longer growth period for the babies in the womb. Marsupials also have an underdeveloped placenta that limits their gestation period.

Developed brains

Placental mammals have all the common traits of mammals. Their body temperature is slightly higher than monotremes and marsupials. Placental mammals have the most developed brains in the animal kingdom and they are the most dominant terrestrial vertebrates. They are found almost everywhere and in various sizes. They may range from small scavengers to herbivores of all sizes or powerful carnivores. Placental mammals include humans, dogs, cats, bears, wolves, beavers, Beluga whales, foxes, bisons and bats.

Which membrane separates the embryo from the mother?

Origin

In July 1997, researchers discovered the fossils of a new mammal—*Maelestes gobiensis*—in the Gobi Desert, Mongolia. It was a fairly complete fossil of a shrew-like animal, but slightly bigger in size. This type of structure was a rarity amongst the early mammals. According to researchers, *Maelestes* was one of the placental mammals that originated around 65 million years ago in the Northern Hemisphere. They existed during the late Cretaceous Period, which was characterized by the presence of dinosaurs such as Velociraptor, Oviraptor and Protoceratops.

Facts
- There are about 4,000 species of placental mammals.
- The different species of placental mammals are divided into 18 orders.

Birth of baby mammals

Placental mammals bear live young that are nourished in the mother's womb before birth. The placenta carries food, oxygen and nourishment from the mother to the child. The young ones of placental mammals are more developed as they are born when they are in an advanced stage. The placenta is made of the same amniotic membrane that surrounds the embryo in the eggs of reptiles, birds and monotreme mammals. The amniotic membrane separates the young embryo from the mother's auto-immune system. The immune system is prone to attacking the child considering it to be a foreign body.

Great Apes

Apes are primates. Most apes live in the tropical and subtropical regions of the Americas, Africa and Asia. There are two groups of apes—the lesser apes and the great apes. The lesser apes include gibbons and siamangs. Gorillas, chimpanzees, bonobos and orangutans are the great apes.

Orangutans

Orangutans are one of the great apes known for their intelligence. They have a bulky body, long arms, short legs and no tail. Their hands and feet are quite similar to those of humans. Orangutans are omnivores that feed on plants, seeds, flowers and small mammals. They live mostly in trees and swing through them using a hand-over-hand motion, but are also able to walk upright for short distances. These animals have a highly developed ability to think and reason. They depend more on their vision than their sense of smell and have a short, broad nose instead of a snout.

Chimpanzees

Chimpanzees are found in dense rainforests, open woodlands and broad grasslands of Africa. They feed on insects, eggs, fruits and even meat. Usually, chimpanzees are called 'chimps'. The colour of their face ranges from pink to black and their body is covered with long, black hair. They either walk normally on all fours or swing from tree to tree. They use the technique of 'knuckle walking'—the soles of the feet and the back joints of fingers support their weight. They are very social animals and live in communities of 20-100 members.

Gorillas

Gorillas live in central Africa. They are the largest apes and the wild male can weigh over 200 kg. Gorillas have two species: eastern and western, which are further divided into subspecies. Their bodies are covered with thick dark hair except for the face, chest, palms and soles of the feet. They are shy and peaceful herbivores that feed on bamboo and leafy plants. They are very intelligent animals and use varied means of communication. A study by scientists has proved that gorillas use 'baby talk' gestures to communicate with their babies. Gorillas are endangered animals and their only natural enemies are humans.

Facts

- Bonobos are great apes that live in the Democratic Republic of the Congo.
- Gorillas build a new nest everyday. They usually do not sleep in the same nest twice.

Chimpanzees are usually called _____.

Gibbons

Gibbons are lesser apes found in Southeast Asia. There are 15 known species of gibbons that range from Northeast India to southern China to Borneo. They are acrobatic mammals that swing gracefully through the trees. They mostly live on trees and rarely descend to the ground. They are tailless and many of them have white markings on the face, hands and feet.

Opposable big toe

A gibbon's body is completely adapted to live among the canopies of the rainforests. Their unusually long arms help them to swing from one branch to another, while their strong muscular legs add the necessary thrust required for long leaps. Some gibbons are known to leap as wide as 15 m. One of their toes is the opposable big toe, which makes it possible for them to grasp the tree branches. Their hands have four fingers and an opposable thumb. Often when they swing, they use the four fingers like a hook to hang by.

Facts

- Gibbons are among the most threatened primates.
- Gibbons can sleep while sitting on tree branches.

Family ties

Unlike most other apes, gibbons are monogamous. Families share a very strong bond and the members strongly defend their territory. They are known for the long, loud songs that they sing together. Mated pairs and even the families sing these songs, the echo of which covers long distances in the forest.

Siamangs

Siamangs are the largest gibbons that weigh up to 13 kg. They inhabit the rainforests of Malaysia, Thailand and Sumatra. These apes are covered with a black, shaggy coat of hair. However, the hair around their mouth and chin is paler. Siamangs can be distinguished by their throat sac, which can be inflated to the size of their head. They use their throat pouch to make loud calls or sing songs. The largest of siamangs can grow up to 1 m.

Which is the largest gibbon in the world?

Flying Mammals: Bats

Bats are the only mammals that can fly. Some mammals can glide, but none except bats can fly using wings. There are over 900 known species of bats. Bats are found almost everywhere apart from the Arctic, Antarctica and a few isolated oceanic islands. Most bats are insectivores. Some species also feed on fruits, nectar and small animals such as lizards frogs. Some bats even eat fish.

Echolocation

Bats use sounds to navigate and detect obstacles in their flight. This technique is known as echolocation. More than half of the bat species use this technique by contracting their larynx to produce echolocation sounds. Some bat species also click their tongue, producing a sound that is represented by hitting two round pebbles together. Most bats produce a long sequence of calls. The higher-pitch sounds give them a greater clarity about the size, range, position, speed and direction of their prey. When the sound hits their prey, it bounces back enabling them to know what lies in front of them.

Facts

- The bumblebee bat is the world's smallest mammal.
- Vampire bats are the only mammals that feed entirely on animal blood.

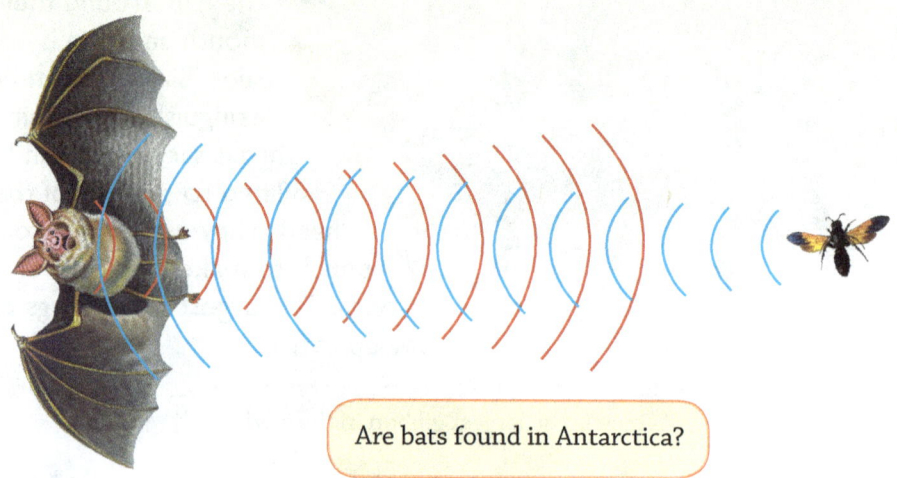

Are bats found in Antarctica?

Beneficial

Bats are highly beneficial animals. A single bat can eat over 3,000 insects in a night. Insectivorous bats can thus help humans to get rid of insects without the use of chemical insecticides. Bats are also great pollinators. Countless plants depend on bats for pollination and seed dispersal.

Adaptations

A bat's wing are modified fingers that contain the same bones as a four-fingered human hand. A thin, strong membrane spreads across these bones, connecting them to the bat's back and legs. The thumb clings to the surface when the bat alights. Many bats can't fly from the ground and have to take off by dropping from a hanging position. When they have to land, they slow down and take hold of a branch or other surface. Some even perform a flip and then take hold of a surface. Bats also have a sophisticated sense of smell, which helps them find fruits and flowers.

Wild Dogs

There are currently 35 species of wild dogs known to us. They belong to the dog family, Canidae, which includes all extinct dog species as well. Members of the family Canidae are known as canids, and may also be referred to as 'canines'. The family of canines include animals like jackals, wolves and foxes. The most well-known wild dog species include the grey wolf, coyote, red fox, Arctic fox, kit fox, African wild dog and golden jackal.

Coyotes

Coyotes (prairie wolves or brush wolves) are the fastest runners of all wild dogs. They can run up to 64 km in an hour. They live in the grassy plains, forests and mountains of North America. Coyotes are highly social animals. They form strong family bonds and live in close-knit groups called packs. A pack usually has a breeding pair and their pups and few other associates. After a female gives birth to babies, both the male and female take care of the pups by feeding and protecting them.

Facts

- Arctic foxes can survive temperatures as low as −58°C.
- Mexican wolves are one of the most endangered species of wolves.

Name the fastest runner of all wild dogs.

Foxes

Foxes are the smallest wild dogs. They have short legs, an elongated narrow muzzle, erect triangular ears, thick fur and a long, bushy tail. They have black triangular markings between the eyes and the nose, and the tip of the tail is often a different colour from the rest of the body. Foxes are found throughout the Americas, Eurasia and Africa, inhabiting mostly forests, chaparral and desert regions. Foxes mostly feed on invertebrates and small mammals, reptiles, amphibians, scorpions, grasses, berries, fruits and more.

Wolves

Wolves are closely related to jackals and domestic dogs. They have strong jaws, powerful legs and bushy tails. They are found in some regions of North America, Europe and Asia. Wolves are highly social animals. They live in packs. The pack consists of a breeding pair—the alpha pair— its offspring and a few unrelated wolves. The members of a pack care for the young together and hunt together. Though wolves are not known to attack humans, they are considered one of the most fearsome members of the animal kingdom.

Wild Cats

Wild cats are carnivorous members of the cat family. The family includes lions, leopards, tigers, pumas and cheetahs, along with many smaller members like caracals, ocelots and wildcats. These wild cats are some of the fiercest predators in the world. Tigers are the largest of all wild cats.

Leopards

Leopards are heavier than cheetahs and have a large head as compared to the rest of their body. They have rosettes rather than spots. Each rosette is made up of three to four spots on the outside with a yellow-brown centre. They are generally found in dense bushes and are the most cunning and stealthy hunters. Their prey ranges from fish to monkeys and baboons. While hunting, they keep a low profile and sink through the grass. Leopards are good climbers and often drag their preys onto trees to hide them.

Tigers

The largest wild cats in the world, tigers are most identified by their reddish-brown and black stripes. They can weigh up to 300 kg and can grow up to be 4 m long. These big cats hunt alone and wait until dark to catch their prey (deer and antelope). They are known to sneak very close to their prey before attacking it and may take days to finish eating their food. Unlike other wild cats, tigers are good swimmers and enjoy soaking in water. These endangered animals are widely hunted for their fur.

Cheetahs

Cheetahs are the world's fastest land mammals. They are smaller than lions and leopards, and are now found mainly in sub-Saharan Africa, plains of Southern Asia, the Middle East and India. Cheetahs have long, muscular and slim legs and 'tear drop' black markings that run down their face. They hide in tall grasses to stalk their prey, such as rabbits, ostrich, antelope and impalas, and then race out to attack.

Lions

Lions, the most familiar of all wild cats, have tawny coats and are the only cats with tufted tails and manes. Only male lions develop manes. The Asiatic lion and the African lion are the only two extant lion species. Lions are the most social cats. They usually live in groups of 15 members on average called prides. A pride consists of adult females and their cubs; it doesn't have more than two adult males. The members of a pride protect the cubs, hunt prey and defend the territory together. Females do most of the hunting in a pride.

Facts

- The Amur tiger (Siberian tiger) is the largest wild cat.
- The jaguar is the third largest cat after the tiger and the lion.

Name the largest wild cat.

Hoofed Mammals

Mammals with hoofs—the horny part of the foot that protects the toes— are known as 'ungulates'. The hoof supports the entire body weight of an ungulate. Common ungulates include cows, buffaloes, goats, pigs, sheep, rhinos, camels, hippopotamuses, giraffes, okapis, horses, zebras, donkeys, elks, deer, antelopes and gazelles.

Zebras

Zebras belong to the same family as horses and asses. Their black-and-white striped coat makes them one of the most easily recognizable animals in the world. Zebras are found only in Africa. There are three species of zebras— plains zebra, Grévy's zebra and mountain zebra. Zebras are social animals that are often seen grazing in herds. A zebra family consists of a male (stallion), many females and their young ones. If a zebra is attacked, the family comes to its rescue and circles the wounded zebra to keep the predator away.

Name two species of camels.

Facts

- One species of wild horse, the Przewalski's horse, is now extinct in the wild.
- The moose is the largest member of the deer family.

Rhinos

Rhinos are large hoofed mammals with a thick protective skin and horns on their nose. There are five living species of rhinos—black, white, Javan, Indian and Sumatran rhinos. The black and the white rhinos are found in Africa, and they have two horns on the nose. The remaining rhino species are found in Asia, and they are one-horned. Rhinos are herbivorous animals. The black, Indian, Sumatran and Javan rhinos feed on leaves, buds, fruits etc., while the white rhinos graze grass. The white rhino is the second largest mammal after elephants.

Camels

Camels live in the dry and desert areas of Northern Africa and Asia. There are three species of camels— dromedary or Arabian (with one hump), Bactrian and wild Bactrian (the latter two with two humps). All the species store fat in their humps. They have paddy hoofs with two toes to prevent them from sinking in the sand. They can break down the fat into water and energy when they require it. This is the reason why camels can travel very long distances without water and survive in extremely hot and arid regions. They are mostly domesticated to provide milk, meat and transport.

Elephants

Elephants are large, four-legged, herbivorous mammals. They have a tough, almost hairless hide, a long flexible trunk, and two ivory tusks growing from their upper jaw. There are only two species of elephant that exist today, the African elephant (Loxodonta africana) and the Asian or Indian elephant (Elephas maximus). Both species of elephants are either threatened or endangered.

Trunk

The long trunk is one of the most outstanding features of an elephant. It serves several purposes. It has two nostrils at its end, which helps in breathing, and the finger-like tip helps pick up things. Elephants also use their trunk for bringing food and water to the mouth, nudging calves and trumpeting warnings.

Tusks

Elephants have a pair of elongated teeth known as tusks that continue to grow throughout their lives. One-third of the tusk, which remains hidden from view, is made of tissue, blood and nerves. The visible portion of the tusk is composed of ivory with an outer layer of enamel. The ivory is very valuable and is used to make fashion accessories, piano keys, knives, etc. It is also the reason why elephants face a threat from poachers.

Intelligent animals

Elephants are one of the most intelligent animals on Earth. Their brain is larger than most animals and they are often said to be as intelligent as dolphins. The elephant brain is similar to a human brain in terms of its structure and complexity. Elephants also have an amazingly strong long-term memory. They use a variety of behavioural tools such as compassion, cooperation, self-awareness and maybe language. They also exhibit behaviour associated with grief.

Facts

- Asian elephants are endangered. There are only about 40,000–50,000 left alive.
- Elephants drink 200 l of water every day.

Name the two species of elephants.

Giraffes

Giraffes are the tallest land animals. Their height may vary from 4 to 6 m. They are hoofed animals that live in the grasslands and savannas of Africa. They roam in small groups of up to 20 members. There are eight subspecies of giraffes.

Diet

Giraffes are cud-chewing herbivorous animals. They feed on leaves, flowers and fruits. One of their main foods is the leaves of acacia trees. Their long necks help them browse through the leaves of these trees. Giraffes are also known to eat soil to fulfill their mineral requirements.

Facts

- Giraffes have two small horn-like knobs on their head. These knobs are called ossicones.
- Giraffes can moo, hiss, grunt and whistle to communicate.

Skin

Giraffes have very beautiful spotted skin. No two giraffes have identical patterns on their skin. Different subspecies have different patterns on their skin. Some have small patches, while others may have large or medium-sized patches. The pattern of the coat remains the same throughout a giraffe's life. However, the colour may change depending on their health.

Height: a disadvantage

Giraffes are so tall that they find it difficult to drink water from water holes. They have to spread their legs and bend their bodies at an awkward angle to reach water holes, which makes them vulnerable to attack from predators such as Africa's big cats. However, they need to drink only once in several days.

Tongue

Giraffes have a long, muscular, prehensile tongue that helps them pluck and eat leaves. A giraffe can extend its tongue up to 21 inches. The tongue may be blue or black in colour. Giraffes spend most of their time eating and travel long distances to forage for food.

What are the horns of a giraffe called?

Giant Pandas

The giant panda is a black-and-white bear that lives in China. It is a large, robust animal with a round head, heavy shoulders, a stocky body and a short tail. It has black fur on its ears, around its eyes, muzzle, legs and shoulders. Giant pandas inhabit the mountain forests in central-western and southwestern China.

Diet

A typical panda spends half its day eating. Giant pandas love to eat bamboos. China has over 700 species of bamboos. Their favourites are umbrella bamboo, arrow bamboo and golden bamboo. Pandas spend 10-16 hours a day eating bamboo and consume between 31 and 45 kg of bamboo in a day.

Mating

Giant pandas are solitary creatures. They use their sharp sense of smell to find females for mating during the spring season. The females give birth to a single cub or two after a five-month pregnancy.

Facts

- Giant pandas are shy animals and do not venture into areas inhabited by humans.
- They are considered a national treasure in China and are provided the highest type of legal protection.

Threatened

Giant pandas are one of the rarest animals on Earth. There are only around 1,800 giant pandas left in the wild, and around 600 pandas live in zoos and breeding centres. They are threatened by the destruction of their habitat. Large areas of China's natural forests have been cleared for agriculture, timber and firewood to meet the needs of the large and growing human population. Other threats include illegal hunting, low reproductive rate and food shortage. The giant pandas in the wild are rarely seen and are considered elusive.

What do pandas like to eat?

Rodents

Rodents constitute the largest family of mammals. The word means 'gnawing animals'. They have two long pairs of incisors that they use as chisels to gnaw on hard food like nuts and wood. The incisors grow continuously and are also usually worn down by gnawing. Squirrels, rats, mice and porcupines belong to the family of rodents.

Capybaras

The capybara is a semi-aquatic mammal found in South America. It is the largest rodent. Agouti, chinchillas, coyphillas, and guinea pigs are closely related to capybaras. It is a good swimmer and can stay underwater for up to five minutes. Capybaras are herbivores and usually feed on grass and other small plants. They are social and are found in groups of 10 to 20 near waterbodies in forested areas.

Facts

- A group of rats is called a mischief.
- The groundhog, also known as woodchuck or whistle-pig, is a large rodent found in North America.

Name the largest rodent.

Beavers

Beavers are large semi-aquatic rodents endemic to North America and Europe. They are the second largest rodent after capybaras. Beavers are known for the large dams that they build in lakes, rivers and streams by felling trees. They are also valued for their fur coat and hunted for their meat. There are two existing species of beavers: the European beaver, found in parts of Europe, and the American beaver or Canadian beaver, found in Canada, the US and parts of Mexico.

Rats

Rats are medium-sized, long-tailed rodents. The term 'rat' usually refers to two main species of house rats—the Norway rat and the roof rat. Both species are endemic to Asia, but have spread throughout the world. Rats are nocturnal, have poor eyesight and are colour-blind. They do not have very developed senses of hearing, smell, taste and touch. They are omnivorous scavengers and eat almost anything—fruit, nuts, reptiles, fish and fungus. Their strong teeth allow them to gnaw through wood, copper and aluminum. Rats are very social and affectionate animals, but are also the carriers of diseases such as plague, rat fever, typhus and meningitis.

Marsupials

Marsupials are mammals that have an external pouch (marsupium) in which the immature young are raised after birth until early infancy. Due to early birth, the young are born undeveloped, and they crawl into the mother's pouch to grow further. Marsupials are found in Australia, Central and South America, New Zealand and on a few islands in the Pacific. Kangaroos, wallabies, koalas and opossums are the most commonly known marsupials.

Evolution

Marsupials and placental mammals branched out from monotremes during the Cretaceous Period. The primitive marsupials had four pairs of molar teeth in each jaw, while the placental mammals didn't have more than three pairs. *Sinodelphys szalayi* is the earliest known marsupial. It lived in China around 125 million years ago. After the division of the supercontinent Pangaea, the marsupials finally found themselves inhabiting Australia. The wide variety of marsupials seen today evolved in Australia. In the recent times, modern marsupials seem to have reached the islands of Borneo or Sulawesi through Australia.

Facts

- A joey that has left its mother's pouch and yet returns to feed on its mother milk is known as a 'young-at-foot'.
- Male adult kangaroos are also called 'boomers'.

What is the other name for the pouch in marsupials?

The pouch

All marsupials do not have a permanent pouch. It is formed by a temporary fold of the skin that swells up to form a sac during the breeding season and disappears after the baby has developed. Usually, carnivorous mammals, such as quolls, dunnarts and phascogales, have a temporary pouch. Inside the pouch, the newborns are permanently attached to the mother's nipple. Once they grow, they leave the pouch and return only when they feel threatened or to sleep. Kangaroos and wallabies allow their young to stay in the pouch even after the young ones are capable of managing on their own. A few marsupials do not have a pouch at all.

Joeys

A baby marsupial is called 'joey' and is only the size of a jelly bean. The baby is born blind, naked and furless. A joey cannot regulate its own body temperature and depends upon external heat. The pouch temperature must constantly be around 30–32°C for the joey to feel comfortable. After the full development, the joey spends long periods outside the pouch to feed itself and learn survival skills.

Different Marsupials

Marsupials can be terrestrial as well as arboreal. Koalas, possums and opossums are arboreal, while kangaroos, wallabies, bandicoots, quolls and bilbies are terrestrial. Kangaroos and wallabies belong to the family of macropods meaning 'big foot'. Most macropods have hind legs larger than their forelimbs and long muscular tails for balance.

Kangaroos

Kangaroos are the largest marsupials. They have large ears on the top of their small heads, a long snout and short arms with clawed fingers. They have very good eyesight and hearing ability. They can even swivel their ears in all directions to pick up sounds. Most kangaroos move about at night in search of food and rest throughout the day. They usually hop from one place to the other.

Koalas

Koalas are often referred to as 'koala bears' due to their bear-like appearance, but they are not really bears. They are herbivorous marsupial mammals found in Australia. They have a thick coat, large ears and long limbs with large, sharp claws to help them climb trees.

Name the smallest wallaroo.

Bandicoots

Bandicoots are small marsupial mammals that live in Australia and the nearby islands. They have long, pointed, shrew-like faces; gray or brown fur; and long, bushy, rat-like tails. Their pouch opens towards the rear to prevent dirt from entering it. They feed on insects, worms, roots and vegetables.

Facts
- When under stress, koalas make a loud cry similar to the cry of a human baby.
- The smallest wallaroo is called the Black wallaroo.

Kangaroo rats

Kangaroo rats are small rodents that live in North America. They are called so because they hop around like kangaroos and look like mice. They have a buff-coloured fur and the their tail is longer than their body. Kangaroo rats are nocturnal. They feed on leaves from saltbush, seeds, insects and fungi.

Wallabies

Wallabies are members of the kangaroo family, but are smaller than them. They are usually small- to medium-sized with powerful hind legs and a tail. When threatened by predators, they use their legs to deliver powerful kicks. Wallabies are classified into three groups based on their habitat: shrub wallabies, brush wallabies, and rock wallabies.

Marine Mammals

Marine mammals display the same characteristics as other mammals. However, their distinct feature is that they have adapted to living all or part of their life in oceans. Most marine mammals have a thick layer of blubber (fat) on their body that keeps them warm in the cold ocean waters. Many species of marine mammals stay underwater for a long time but come to the surface to breathe.

Sirenians are also known as _____.

Cetaceans

All whales, dolphins and porpoises are cetaceans. They may be as small as the Hector's dolphin (120 cm) or as large as the blue whale (30 m). The evidence from fossils show that cetaceans and land-dwelling mammals shared common ancestors. Some species of cetaceans are known for their high intelligence. The behaviour and distribution of different species of cetaceans vary greatly. Many whales and other cetaceans do not chew but swallow their entire prey.

Polar bears

Polar bears are the world's largest bears and they live in the Arctic region. Though most polar bears are born on land, they spend most part of their life at seas. They have webbed feet and are known to be excellent swimmers. They are endangered because their habitat is shrinking due to the melting sea ice. The feed on seals, which make up most of their diet.

Sirenians

Also known as 'sea cows', sirenians consist of dugongs and three species of manatees. They are found in the inland waterways and coastal areas of the US, Central and South America, West Africa, Asia and Australia. All sea cow species are endangered. Though sirenians appear fat, they are highly muscular and have dense bones.

Facts

- The female polar bear is half the size of the male.
- Sea otters float on their back and open mollusks by smashing them on a stone balanced on their chest.

Pinnipeds

Pinnipeds, such as seals, sea lions and walruses are found all over the world. They are fin-footed mammals and have flippers on their front and rear. Pinnipeds are divided into three families: the earless or true seals, the fur seals and walruses. These three families contain 33 species altogether.

Monotremes

Monotremes are rare egg-laying mammals found in Australia and New Guinea. There are only three living species of monotremes: platypus and two species of the spiny anteater. The word 'monotreme' means, one opening, it refers to the presence of only one opening in these animals for getting rid of waste and laying eggs.

Platypuses

The platypus looks like a unique mix of many animals. It has a tail like a beaver's, a body like an otter's, a walk like a reptile's and webbed feet and beak like a duck's—the webbing is more prominent in the front feet. Its broad body and flat tail are covered with a dense brown waterproof fur to trap heat inside the body. Platypuses are carnivores that feed on small creatures like crayfish, worms, snails and shrimps. They can store food in the cheek pouches while hunting underwater.

Facts

- Male platypuses have a spur on one hind foot that excretes venom.
- The spiny anteaters can live up to 50 years in captivity.

The platypus has waterproof fur. True/False?

Eggs

The eggs of monotremes remain within the mother's body for some time. They do not have a placenta, but the egg shell is porous, enabling the absorption of the mother's nutrients. The gestation period is 10–12 days. The young ones hatch by tearing the shell with the help of a temporary egg tooth on their snout. When they have fully hatched, the newborns start feeding on their mother's milk. Even after they grow up, the infants are under the protective care of the parents for a long period of time.

Spiny anteaters

Spiny anteaters are covered with coarse hair and spines resembling a porcupine. They have a long, slender snout that functions as the nose and mouth. When a spiny anteater finds itself in danger, it either digs a burrow and hides in it or rounds itself up into a spiny ball. They feed on ants and termites.

Glossary

Ancestor: an organism who has lived years ago and modern forms have evolved from it

Beneficial: something that has a good effect

Bipedal: refers to animals that walk on two legs

Chaparral: a wide land with different types of terrains, such as flat plains, rocky hills and mountain slopes, and has a very hot and dry climate

Destruction: damaging something to such an extent that it stops existing

Dominant: important or powerful

Endangered Animal: animals that are on the verge of becoming extinct

Evaporation: the process through which a liquid converts into steam or gas

Extinct: refers to an organism that is dead or no longer exist

Fossil: the decayed remains of ancient plants and animals buried deep inside the earth since millions of years ago

Gestation Period: the time period in which a baby develops inside its mother till its birth

Gnaw: to nibble or keep biting something

Grassland: a large piece of land where wild grass grows

Habitat: the natural home of an organism

Illegal: something which is against the rules and guidelines of a governing body

Immune System: a body's defence system that fights off germs and infections

Inhabit: to reside in a particular place or environment

Monogamous: having only one mate at a time

Muzzle: the nose and mouth of an animal such as dog

Navigate: steer the way or to find the path

Nocturnal: to be active at night

Nourish: to supply with nutrients

Ocelot: an endangered wild cat of america that has a yellow fur with black spots

Pollination: the process of spreading of pollens (the dust of flowers) through wind, insects or animals in order to produce new seeds

Primitive: very old

Quadruped: an organism that walks on four legs

Savanna: a grassland with small trees

Scavenger: an organism that feeds on the dead remains of other organisms

Terrestrial: relating to the earth

Threatened: on the verge of becoming endangered

Vertebrate: an organism with a backbone

Woodland: a large piece of land covered with trees

Answers

Page No. 8 *Sinodelphys* and *Andrewsarchus*

Page No. 11 Yes

Page No. 13 Age of Mammals

Page No. 14 Amniotic membrane

Page No. 17 Chimps

Page No. 19 Siamang

Page No. 20 No

Page No. 22 Coyotes

Page No. 25 Amur tiger

Page No. 26 Dromedary and Bactrian

Page No. 29 Asian and African elephants

Page No. 31 Ossicones

Page No. 33 Bamboo

Page No. 34 Capybara

Page No. 36 Marsupium

Page No. 38 The Black wallaroo

Page No. 40 Sea cows

Page No. 42 True

PRIMATES

Introduction

Primates are one of the more diverse groups of mammals. They include humans, apes, monkeys, tarsiers and non-tarsier prosimians such as lemurs, lorises, galagos, etc.
There are 376–524 species of primates. Primates are found in Africa, Asia and South and Central America.

They range in size from a mountain gorilla that weighs 160 kg to a pygmy marmoset that weighs 100 g. Primates have large brains, grasping hands and feet, and nails instead of claws. They are the closest relatives of humans; however, they are under threat due to the destruction of their habitat.

Types of Primates

All primates are classified into two basic groups, Strepsirrhini and Haplorhini. The group Strepsirrhini includes lemurs, lorises and galagos, while Haplorhini includes tarsiers, monkeys and apes. Before this classification was accepted, primates were classified into prosimians and anthropoids. However, the old classification is rarely used now.

Strepsirrhini traits

The name Strepsirrhini was put forth by Étienne Geoffroy Saint-Hilaire, a French naturalist. The members of this group are characterized by wet, naked nostrils, whiskers, large ears and large reflective eyes that are adapted for a nocturnal life. They also have a highly developed sense of smell and special scent glands that allow non-verbal communication.

Haplorhini traits

The first haplorhines evolved around 50 million years ago. The members of this group are characterized by dry and rounded nostrils, a free upper lip that is not attached to the gum, a larger brain and a longer lifespan.

Social animals

The most social of animals, primates are often seen in pairs or groups. They have a family structure and female primates also take good care of their babies. The males are known to defend their territory against challengers. Many primate groups split up during the day to forage for food but return at night to sleep with their group.

Facts

- The first primate-like animal evolved about 70 million years ago.
- Prosimians have light-reflecting eyes.

What are the two major groups of primates?

Lemurs

The word lemur means 'spirits of the dead' in Latin. There are about 50 known species of lemurs. They are arboreal and spend most of their time in trees. Lemurs come in different sizes depending on their species. Mouse lemurs, ring-tailed lemurs and red ruffed lemurs are the most commonly known lemurs. Most lemurs are omnivores that feed on leaves, fruits and insects. Some are herbivores and prefer only plants.

Mouse Lemurs

With a weight less than 113.39 g, mouse lemurs are the smallest members of the lemur family. They are only 7–12 cm long. Their body is covered with soft, thick and woolly hair. Their tail is as long as their body. Almost 35 per cent of their body weight is composed of the weight of their long tail and strong hind legs. These lemurs are native to Madagascar.

Red ruffed lemurs

Red ruffed lemurs are characterized by a large body and tail. They are red or brown in colour with a black head, tail, stomach and feet. Their body extends up to a length of 50–55 cm and they weigh up to 5 kg. Red ruffed lemurs are known to produce six infants at a time, usually twins.

Ring-tailed lemurs

Ring-tailed lemurs, also known as **Lemur catta** are medium-sized lemurs. They weigh between 3–4 kg. They have a long tail with alternate black and white rings. These lemurs live in groups of 15–20 individuals with dominant females. Ring-tailed lemurs enjoy sunbathing for many hours by sitting on the ground facing the sun with their arms outspread.

Which is the smallest member of the lemur family ?

Facts

- Lemurs are among the most endangered primates.
- Indri lemurs are the largest living lemurs.

Lorises

Lorises can be found in the forests of India and Sri Lanka. They also inhabit some other parts of South-East Asia. There are eight species of lorises, some of which are tailless while some have a short tail. They are arboreal and nocturnal primates. Lorises, pottos and galagos belong to the same family. While pottos and lorises are slow-movers, galagos move quickly.

Galagos

Galagos (bushbabies) are small primates, usually the size of a squirrel. They live in habitats with trees surrounded by little grass. Their diet varies according to the season. They feed mainly on insects, flowers and fruits during the rainy season. In the dry season, they usually prefer raisins as the other food becomes scarce.

Pottos

Pottos are also known as 'softly-softly' for their slow and smooth movement. They are native to the thickly vegetated areas of Africa. They are small and usually grow up to 30–39 cm in length and weigh about 1.6 kg. Pottos have the ability to remain still for hours to escape the attention of their attackers. They have spiny bones on the upper back shielded by a horny skin, which they use to attack if they are confronted.

> How many species of lorises are there?

Features of lorises

Lorises are broadly classified into slender and slow lorises. These primates are identified by their huge eyes with dark patches around them as well as their short index fingers. Their arms and legs are of the same length. They have a grey or brown fur. They have a long claw on the second toe, also known as the grooming claw, which they use for combing and cleaning their fur. Lorises are known for their comic postures.

Facts

- Loris is the Dutch word for 'clown'. Lorises were named for their funny faces after they were discovered by European explorers.
- Bushbabies are giant leapers. They are known to cover a distance of 9 m in seconds.

Tarsiers

Tarsiers are very small, rat-sized primates found in the islands of Southeast Asia. All tarsiers are nocturnal and have big eyes, which enhance their vision at night. Tarsiers are arboreal animals, and they are good leapers. Tarsiers are usually found in groups; however, some tarsiers prefer to be alone. They are known to produce a variety of sounds and have an excellent hearing ability.

Classification

There are three distinct species of tarsiers—Philippine tarsiers, western tarsiers and spectral tarsiers. The Philippine tarsier is also the world's second-mallest known primate. It is native to the southeastern Philippine Islands.

What do they look like?

Tarsiers have a small body covered with a soft fur that is generally brown in colour. They have naked tails that are longer than their body. They are characterized by their finger-like claws and padded hands, which are used to grip tree branches. They have long hind legs.

Big-eyed

Tarsiers have very big eyes. Their eye-to-body ratio is the largest among all mammals. Their eye sockets are even larger than their brain and stomach. They are unable to rotate their eyes. However, they are capable of rotating their head by 360 degrees, which helps them to see behind them.

> Name the three species of tarsiers.

Endangered

The majority of tarsier species are endangered; in fact, some of them are critically endangered. Some of the threats they face are habitat destruction, hunting and human disturbance. These shy animals prefer to be away from humans and they don't live well in captivity.

Facts

- Tarsiers can leap distances up to 5.4 m (18 ft.).
- Tarsiers capable of turning their heads nearly 180° in each direction, allowing them the ability to rotate their heads almost 360°.

Monkeys

Monkeys are higher primates that are known for their well-developed brains and high level of intelligence. There are approximately 200 species of monkeys known today. They are categorized into two groups—Old World monkeys and New World monkeys. New World monkeys are found in the tropical rainforests of South and Central America, Asia and Africa. Old World monkeys are found in the terrestrial habitats of Africa and Asia.

New World monkeys

These monkeys are characterized with a broad, flat nose and a prehensile tail. Their nostrils are far apart and side-facing. They are different from Old World monkeys due to the presence of three premolars instead of two.

Old World monkeys

These monkeys are characterized by a longer snout with downward or forward-facing nostrils, a non-prehensile tail, opposable thumbs and thick pads on their rump. They are usually larger than New World monkeys, and some even have cheek pouches. They may live on trees or on the ground.

Families

There are around 138 species of Old World monkeys. Some of the most common families of Old World monkeys include colobus monkeys, langurs, macaques, mangabeys, baboons and mandrills.

Five Families

New World monkeys are divided into five families—marmosets and tamarins; capuchin and squirrel monkeys; night or owl monkeys; titis, sakis and uakaris; and howler, spider, woolly spider and woolly monkeys.

Facts

- Monkeys are known to have an IQ level of 174 and are capable of solving many complex problems.
- The monkey appears as the ninth animal in the Chinese Zodiac.

How many families of New World monkeys are there?

Capuchin and Squirrel Monkeys

Capuchin and squirrel monkeys are members of the New World family. They are found in parts of South and Central America. The members of both the monkey families are primarily arboreal and rarely come down to the ground. They are usually small in size and have typical wide, flat noses.

Intelligent

Capuchin monkeys are considered to be very intelligent monkeys. These animals are trained and used in many countries to aid physically handicapped or partially or completely paralyzed people. Often, they are also trained to perform tricks and used for entertainment.

Capuchin monkeys

Capuchin monkeys can be easily recognized by the typical colouring of their coat. Their face, neck and shoulders are covered with light tan or cream-coloured fur, while the back of their head and the rest of the body are marked by a dark brown coat. Like most other primates, these monkeys are social and usually live in large groups. They often give out a variety of calls, like screams, whistles and barks, to communicate with the other members of a group.

Squirrel monkeys

Squirrel monkeys, as their name suggests, are similar to squirrels in appearance. Their body is covered with thick and brightly coloured fur. The colour of the skin around the lips and nostrils is black. Their long tail has a black tip.

Where are capuchin and squirrel monkeys found?

Facts

- Jaguars and falcons hunt capuchin monkeys.
- Male capuchin monkeys urinate on themselves to attract female capuchins.

Woolly, Spider and Howler Monkeys

Howler, spider, woolly and woolly spider monkeys are found in the forests of Central and South America. They are small- to medium-sized monkeys with a long prehensile tail and dark body. There are 15 species of howler, seven species of spider, two species of woolly spider and five species of woolly monkeys. Spider, woolly and howler monkeys are omnivores, while woolly spider monkeys are herbivores.

Spider monkeys

The acrobats of the world of monkeys, spider monkeys spend most of their time leaping from one tree to another in the tropical forests of Mexico and Brazil. They have unusually long arms with long fingers and a short thumb. They have a long prehensile tail, which acts as a fifth limb and also supports their weight when they walk on the ground.

Howler monkeys

One of the largest of New World monkeys, the howler monkey is named so because of its loud howling calls. Howler monkeys are characterized by a beard and long, thick hair, which may be black, brown or red. They are social and live in groups of 10–20 monkeys. They communicate with the members of their group and other groups by howling. When a group of howlers start howling together, their cries can be heard as far as 4.8 km.

Woolly monkeys

Woolly monkeys are named so because of the thick and woolly coat of fur that covers their body. They are large, muscular monkeys characterized by potbellies. They have a long thick tail with a strong grip. Their tail can be longer than the length of their head and body combined.

Are woolly spider monkeys carnivores?

Facts

- The black spider monkey is one of the largest primates of South America.
- Howler monkeys are the loudest land animals.

Baboons

Baboons are one of the largest old world monkeys. These terrestrial monkeys are found in Africa. They can be easily recognized by their long dog-like muzzle and close-set eyes. Their sharp canine teeth are similar to those of dogs, and their body is covered with an ash-grey fur. There are five different species of baboons—olive, chacma, yellow, guinea and hamadryas.

Chacma baboons

Chacma baboons are the largest of all baboons. They are found from South Africa, north to Angola, Zambia and Mozambique. These baboons are generally dark brown to grey in colour and have a downward sloping face. They can also be distinguished from the other species by the absence of a mane. Male chacma baboons are larger than the females.

Facts
- The hamadryas baboon was considered to be sacred by the ancient Egyptians.
- Baboons can survive without water for a long period of time.

Behaviour

Baboons are usually found in large groups. A group has a complex structure with several levels of hierarchy. The members of a group spend most of their time grooming each other. Baboons are very vocal and communicate by grunting, screaming and barking. A new research has shown that the top-ranking males in a baboon group experience high stress levels because they are expected to keep their territory safe at all times.

Hamadryas baboons

Hamadryas baboons are found in rocky semi-desert areas of Northeast Africa and the Arabian Peninsula. Some of these baboons may be found at altitudes up to 2,v600 m. The males have a fluffy mane and are grey in colour, while the females are olive brown in colour and lack the mane.

Name the five species of baboons.

Mandrills and Drills

Mandrills and drills are closely related to each other. Mandrills are the most colourful primates. Drills have a similar appearance, but they lack the colourful faces. Both species are found in the rainforests and grasslands of Africa. They are semi-terrestrial and may climb trees at night to sleep.

Colourful primates

Mandrills have a hairless face marked with red nostrils and lips, a golden beard, and white patches on either side of the nose. The underside of a mandrill's body is also brightly coloured. They have a white belly and a bright red and blue rump. Male mandrills are more brightly coloured than female and young mandrills. The colours of a mandrill's body brighten up when it is excited or angry.

Behaviour

Mandrills live in large groups. A group may consist of up to 20 members. The male with the brightest colours is chosen as the leader. In general, mandrills are noisy and violent in nature. They communicate using various kinds of sounds and scent markings. Often they shake their head and bare their teeth as a friendly gesture.

Endangered drills

Drills are one of the most endangered primates of Africa. Deforestation and hunting are the two primary threats that these animals are facing at an increased rate. Drills are found in the forests of Nigeria and Cameroon and on the Bioko Island in the Gulf of Guinea. These short-tailed monkeys look similar to mandrills, but their face does not have bright blue and red colours as seen in mandrills.

Facts

- Mandrills are the largest monkey in the world.
- Special pouches in their mouths allow the mandrills to store food for later.

When do the colours of a mandrill's body brighten up?

Macaques

Macaques are old world monkeys found across Asia and Africa. They are the most common primates on the planet after human beings. There are 23 known species of the macaque family. Macaques, like most primates, live in large social groups with a complex social hierarchy.

Snow monkeys

The Japanese macaque, also known as the snow monkey, is native to Japan. Besides humans, it is the most northern-living primate. These macaques are perhaps one of the most intelligent primates. During a study conducted on them, it was found that they are the only animals that wash their food before eating it. They are also known for their hot spring baths. In the winter, when temperatures are below the freezing point, many of these animals visit hot springs to warm up.

Barbary macaques

These are tailless macaques found in the mountainous forests of Morocco, Algeria and Gibraltar. They are also often referred to as Barbary apes because of their missing tail. They are the only macaques found outside Asia. They live in large social groups of up to more than 80 members and communicate using a variety of calls like pants, screams and barks.

Rhesus macaques

The rhesus is one of the most common species of macaques. These monkeys are usually grey or brown in colour and have a red face and rump. They have close cropped hair on their head. They are both arboreal and terrestrial and are excellent swimmers as well. Rhesus monkeys are most commonly found near human habitats. They are omnivorous and feed on seeds, fruits, leaves, cereals and small insects.

Facts

- Barbary macaques sleep in clusters of two to three animals.
- In the winter, Japanese macaques sleep on trees to prevent themselves from being buried in snow.

How many species of macaques are there?

Colobuses, Langurs and Doucs

Colobuses, langurs and odd-nosed monkeys belong to the same family. These medium-sized Old World monkeys are native to Africa and Asia. Most of these monkeys have adapted themselves to different habitats, ranging from mountain forests to grasslands and mangroves.

Endangered doucs

Doucs or douc langurs are a kind of odd-nosed monkeys. They live in the forests of Vietnam, Laos and Cambodia. Their body is grey in colour. They have a white face and throat and a rust-coloured necklace on the chest. Their thighs are black, while the lower legs are rust-coloured. The red-shanked douc langur and the black-shanked douc langur are the two main douc species. Doucs are on the verge of extinction due to the destruction of their habitat.

Doucs are not endangered. (True/False)

Proboscis monkeys

The proboscis monkey is a strange-looking potbellied monkey with a big odd nose. Males have a longer nose than the females. Proboscis monkeys are native to Borneo.

Langurs

Langurs, also known as leaf-eating monkeys, can be easily recognized by their long tail, slender body and dark face. There are three types of langurs—the grey langur, surilis and lutungs. Grey langurs are the most common langurs. There are seven known species of grey langurs. Surilis are small langurs found in Sumatra, Borneo and Java, while lutungs are found in India, Sri Lanka, Thailand, Java, Bali, Borneo and parts of China.

Facts

- The word 'langur' means 'long tail'.
- Grey langurs are considered sacred by the Hindus.

Apes

Apes are tailless primates that are closely related to humans. There are two types of apes—great apes and lesser apes. Gorillas, orangutans, chimpanzees and bonobos belong to the group of great apes. Gibbons and siamangs are known as lesser apes because they are smaller in size and have smaller brains.

Apes and monkeys

Until some time back, apes and monkeys were considered to be very similar. However, this is not the case. Apes do not have tails like monkeys, who use their tail for balance. Apes are also much bigger than monkeys barring gibbons, some of which are smaller in size than some monkeys. Apes are also believed to be more intelligent than monkeys.

Evolution

Scientists believe that the first apes evolved from Old World monkeys, about 24—34 million years ago. Gibbons were the first to evolve about 18 million years ago, while orangutans appeared about 14 million years ago.

Gibbons are great apes. True/False?

Big and smart

Apes are usually bigger than other primates and most of them can walk on two legs if required. They are also known to have high levels of intelligence, with some having developed the skills to use tools and the ability to solve puzzles. Some researches have shown that chimpanzees can top college students in basic memory tests and other skills. They can even communicate using sign language.

Facts

- Nakalipithecus nakayamai was an early species of apes that lived in Kenya about 10 million years ago.
- Kamoyapithecus was a primate that lived in Africa about 24.2—27.5 million years ago.

Gorillas

Gorillas are known as the largest living primates. They are found in the tropical and subtropical forests of Central Africa. Gorillas are heavy and strong animals. They have a dark skin covered with black or brown hair. They are characterized by a huge head and a bulging forehead that protects their eyes. Their stomach is larger than their chest due to the presence of enlarged intestines. Their human-like arms are longer than their legs.

Types

There are two species of gorillas—western gorillas and eastern gorillas. Eastern gorillas are the larger of the two and western gorillas have a fur that is lighter in colour. Both these species are found in the equatorial forests of Africa, and their territories are divided by the Congo Basin forest. Each species has two subspecies.

▲ *Western gorilla*

▲ *Eastern gorilla*

Behaviour

Gorillas spend most of their day travelling and finding food. They are also known to build different nests for night and day. Day nests are simple, while night nests are usually big. Gorillas build a new nest everyday. Baby gorillas share the nest with their mother until they are about three, after which they build their own nest. Gorillas use a variety of calls and expressions to communicate. When angry or excited, a gorilla may stand upright on two legs and beat its chest.

Social life

Gorillas, like most primates, are social animals that live in groups. A group size may range from 5–50 individuals. The territory occupied by a group depends on its size. Often one or more groups may occupy the same area. A group is led by a silverback. Silverbacks are mature adult males. They are named so because of the patch of silver grey hair on their back. When female gorillas mature, they usually leave their group to find a mate and form a new group. Male gorillas stay back in the group.

Facts

- Every gorilla has a unique fingerprint.
- The Cross River gorilla, a subspecies of the western gorilla, is the rarest ape in the world.

How many species of gorillas are there?

Chimpanzees

Chimpanzees are found in Africa. They are very intelligent animals and possess the ability to solve complex problems. Chimps are omnivorous and feed on both plant and animal matter. There are two types of chimpanzees—common chimpanzees and pygmy chimpanzees.

Common chimpanzees

Chimpanzees have a thick body covered with long and black hair. However, they have no hair on their face, ears, hands and toes. Their face is pale pink in colour. They have an elongated snout and a white beard. They possess prominent ears and human-like eyes. Infant chimps have a pink-coloured skin when they are born, which turns black as they grow.

Pygmy chimpanzees

The Pygmy chimpanzees, also known as bonobos, are similar to common chimpanzees in appearance. However, they are shorter and weigh less than common chimpanzees. Unlike common chimpanzees, they have a black face and their hair is parted in the middle.

Amazing apes

Chimpanzees are the first group of animals after human beings that can work with simple tools. They use sticks to dig the ground and obtain food like termites, ants and eggs from the nest. Chimpanzees communicate with each other through a system of vocal sounds and hand gestures. They use facial expressions and body language to display their emotions such as affection, sorrow, hilarity, hurt, etc. They have strong sense organs.

What is the other name for pygmy chimpanzees?

Facts

- A chimpanzee named Ham orbited the earth in 1961 and helped test space travel for human astronauts.
- Chimpanzees are five to eight times stronger than human beings.

Orangutans

Orangutan is a Malay word that means 'man of the forest'. Orangutans live in Southeast Asia, particularly in the tropical rainforests of Borneo and Sumatra. They are omnivorous and feed on fruits, leaves and insects. Unlike other primates, orangutans prefer to stay alone.

Largest arboreal primates

Orangutans are the world's largest arboreal mammals. They spend most of their time in trees. Their arms are powerful and longer than their legs. The arms when stretched sideways measure up to 2.1 cm. Their hands have long hook-like fingers and an opposable thumb, which helps them to grasp branches and swing swiftly between treetops.

What do they look like?

Orangutans have a large head and bulky body. They are sometimes known as the 'red ape' due to their orange-brown hair. Orangutans are characterized by a large throat pouch and large fleshy cheek pads on the face. It is through this throat pouch that they produce 'long calls' that can travel a distance of 1.6 km.

Name the two types of orangutans.

Facts
- Orangutans are two-thirds the size of gorillas.
- Orangutans make a new nest each evening to sleep in.

Types

There are two types of orangutans—Sumatran orangutans and Bornean orangutans. Their physical appearance helps to establish the difference between them. Bornean orangutans are larger, while Sumatran orangutans have slender bodies. They have a lightweight body covered with light cinnamon-coloured fur. In contrast, Bornean orangutans have a heavier body that is covered with a dark red-brown fur. Moreover, they have forward-facing cheek pads, unlike the flat sideways cheek pads of the Sumatrans.

Gibbons

Gibbons belong to the group of lesser apes. They have slender, lightweight bones and long arms. They are excellent arm swingers and are thus known as the world's greatest acrobats. Gibbons live in the tropical rainforests of Southeast Asia. They are omnivorous and prefer to live in a forest canopy where food is abundant.

What do they look like?

The lightweight body of gibbons is covered with a soft, thick fur whose colour ranges from black to silver grey. Gibbons are characterized by a small, round bare face that is surrounded by a distinct white hairy band. They can sleep in an upright position due to the presence of skin pads on the lower side of their body.

Types

There are 11 different species of gibbons. These are agile, crested, red-cheeked, hoolock, kloss, lar, white-cheeked, Javan, Bornean, pileated and siamang gibbons. Lar gibbons are the most unusual-looking gibbons and siamang gibbons are the largest gibbons.

Communication and behaviour

Gibbons are sometimes referred to as 'singing apes.' They produce long calls that can be heard up to 3.2 km. Their calls are melodious and produced in a rhythmic tone. They make calls to mark their territories and to communicate with their family members. Gibbons are social animals that live in small groups. They are more active during the day and, like other apes, groom each other.

Facts

- Borneo gibbons' territorial calls often lead poachers to their location.
- When on ground, gibbons walk on two legs.

Gibbons are sometimes also known as _____.

Siamangs

Siamangs are the largest gibbons. They are found in the rainforests of Malaysia and Indonesia. These large gibbons are characterized by a body covered with a thick coat of black fur, white cheeks and long and strong arms. Siamangs are capable of grasping things using both hands and feet. Their hands have four fingers and a smaller opposable thumb. Their feet also have five toes with their big toe as the opposable one.

Social life

Siamangs form strong family bonds. They mate for life and a typical family consists of an adult male and a female and their babies. Male siamangs make great fathers, which is very unlike the other primates. They help the female raise the baby and take care of its needs. The babies stay with their family until they are about five-to-seven years old, and then they venture out to form their own families. Different families form small groups and find food together. During the day, they often sit in pairs to groom each other or huddle together on trees and rest.

Which is the largest gibbon?

Diet

Siamangs are omnivores that forage for fruits, plants and small animals in the forests during the day. Seventy-five percent of their diet consists of leaves, flowers, seeds, tree barks and plant shoots. The remaining includes insects, spiders, bird eggs and small birds.

Facts

- Siamangs do not make 'sleeping nests' unlike most other apes. .
- Siamangs have a grey or pink throat sac.

Calls

Siamangs make the loudest calls of all gibbons. They have a large throat sac that blows up like a balloon to amplify the calls. Male and female siamangs can be easily distinguished by their calls. Males scream or boom, while females make a series of booms and barks. Siamangs are known for their duet songs, which usually involve the adult male and female. A song lasts for about 18 seconds and is usually repeated for 15 minutes.

Threat to Primates

Like many other animals, primates also face the threat of extinction. The International Union for Conservation of Nature (IUCN) lists almost 48 percent of the 634 known species of primates as threatened with extinction. Twenty-five species, which include 11 from Asia, five from Madagascar, six from Africa and three from Central and South America, have been listed as highly threatened and are on the verge of extinction.

Threat from humans

The biggest threat that primates face is from one of their closest relatives—human beings. For years, humans have been ruthlessly destroying their natural habitat by clearing forests and making space for their own use. The loss of natural habitat has forced many of these animals to move to areas populated by humans where they often raid fields for food and as a result are shot by farmers. Many primates are hunted for their meat.

Golden-headed langurs

The golden-headed langur, found on the island of Cat Ba in the Gulf of Tonkin, Vietnam, is probably the most endangered of all primates. There are less than 50 Cat Ba langurs left alive. Since the reproductive rate of these langurs is very low, conservationists believe that it would be very difficult to save them from extinction.

> The biggest threats primates face is from _____.

Facts

- Sumatran orangutans are one of the most critically endangered primates of the world.
- Diseases contracted from humans are also one of the major threats to primates.

Illegal trading

Illegal bushmeat trading poses a significant threat to primates. Baby primates are an easy catch and are among the most desired primates. Poachers kill the mother first so that catching the infant primate becomes easy. Many primates are caught and sold illegally in the pet trade.

Glossary

Abundant: a very large quantity of something

Acrobat: one who can perform skillful feats by balancing one's body

Aid: to help

Arboreal: living on trees

Canopy: a blanket-like covering of branchy trees and leaves that blocks the sunlight from reaching the ground

Conservationist: a person who works to protect the wildlife and environment

Deforestation: to clear the forest areas for commercial purposes

Endangered Animal: an animal who is on the verge of becoming extinct

Extinction: the state of being completely wiped out

Grassland: a wide area of land where wild grass grows

Groom: to clean oneself or another

Habitat: a place where a particular organism lives

Handicap: to be physically disabled

Hierarchy: a system in which animals are placed in ranks according to their age and size

Illegal: an act that is not approved by the government

Indigenous: an organism living only at a particular place

Infant: a newborn baby

Mangrove: a tree that grows near water and its roots grow above the ground

Mature: to become older or to age

Melodious: something that is pleasing to the ears

Muzzle: the nose and mouth of an animal

Nocturnal: to be active at night

Opponent: someone who is competing against another

Opposable Thumb: a thumb that is opposite to the fingers, like the human thumb

Peninsula: a landmass surrounded by water on three sides

Posture: the position of the body while sitting or standing

Prehensile Tail: a tail that can get hold of objects

Premolar: a tooth located behind the canines and in front of the molars, suitable for crushing food

Raisin: a grape that has been dried

Rump: the part of an animal's body above its hind legs or the bottom of an animal

Sacred: related to god or divine

Scarce: not existing in large quantities

Slender: lean and thin

Territory: an area of land that is dominated by a particular group of animals

Tropical Rainforest: a forest that remains green throughout the year, is located near the equator, and has a wet and warm climate

Answers

Page No. 51 — Strepsirrhini and Haplorhini

Page No. 53 — Mouse lemur

Page No. 54 — Eight

Page No. 56 — Philippine tarsiers, western tarsiers and spectral tarsiers

Page No. 59 — Five

Page No. 61 — South and Central America

Page No. 63 — No

Page No. 65 — Olive, chacma, yellow, guinea and hamadryas

Page No. 67 — When they're excited or angry

Page No. 69 — 22

Page No. 70 — False

Page No. 72 — False

Page No. 75 — Two

Page No. 77 — Bonobos

Page No. 78 — Sumatran and Bornean orangutans

Page No. 81 — Singing apes

Page No. 82 — Siamang gibbons

Page No. 84 — Human beings

www.ingramcontent.com/pod-product-compliance
Lightning Source LLC
Chambersburg PA
CBHW050657160426
43194CB00010B/1984